Rookie
Read-About® Math

Apple Fractions

By Donna Townsend

Consultant
Linda Bullock
Math Curriculum Specialist

Children's Press®
A Division of Scholastic Inc.
New York   Toronto   London   Auckland   Sydney
Mexico City   New Delhi   Hong Kong
Danbury, Connecticut

Designer: Herman Adler Design
Photo Researcher: Caroline Anderson
The photo on the cover shows an apple divided into parts.

Library of Congress Cataloging-in-Publication Data

Townsend, Donna.
  Apple fractions / by Donna Townsend.
    p. cm. — (Rookie read-about math)
  Includes bibliographical references and index.
  ISBN 0-516-24419-1 (lib. bdg.)   0-516-24670-4 (pbk.)
  1. Fractions—Juvenile literature. I. Title. II. Series.
  QA117.T69 2004
  513.2'6—dc22
                                    2004005022

5 6 7 8 9 10 R 13 12 11   62

Apples taste so good.

You might want to share
an apple.

You can cut one into parts.

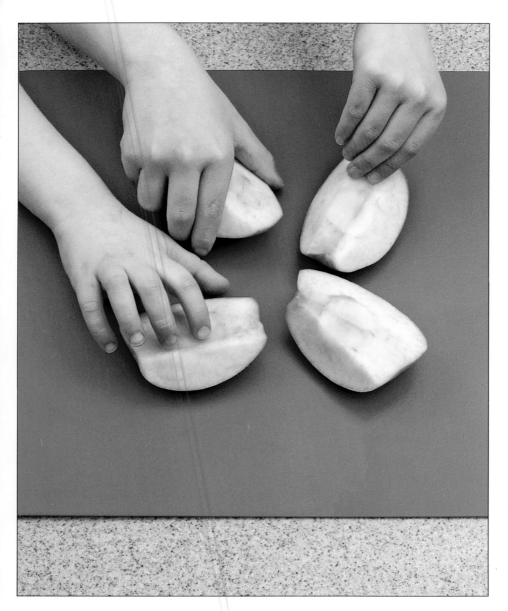

What is a part of
something called?

The part is called
a fraction.

A fraction is a kind of number. It names a part.

This girl is eating a fraction of the apple.

1/2   1/2

This apple is cut in 2 parts. Each part is the same size.

The fraction for each part is 1/2.

This apple is cut in 3 parts.
Each part is the same size.

The fraction for each part
is 1/3.

1/3   1/3   1/3

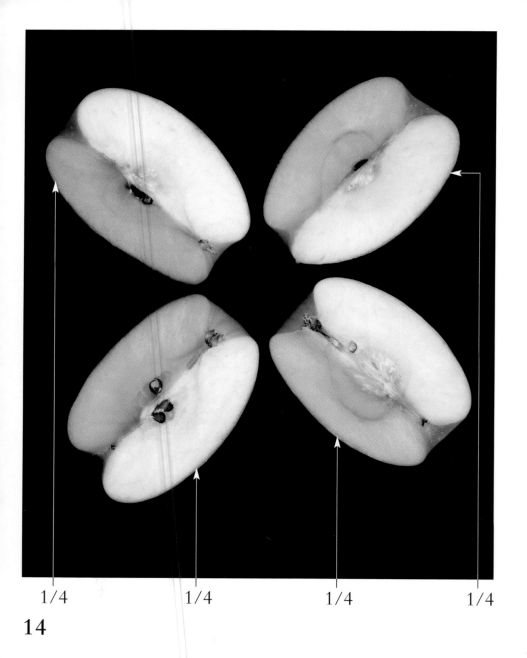

1/4   1/4   1/4   1/4

14

This apple is cut in 4 parts.
Each part is the same size.

The fraction for each part
is 1/4.

What happened to
the apples?

18

Mmmmm. Someone
used the apples to make
apple muffins.

There are 4 muffins on the plate. Don't eat them all at once!

1/4

Take 1 muffin from the plate. You have 1 of the 4 muffins.

What fraction do you have? The fraction for 1 muffin is 1/4.

Give a muffin to a friend.
Together, you have 2 of
the 4 muffins.

What fraction is that?
The fraction for 2 muffins
is 2/4.

1/4   1/4

1/4 + 1/4 = 2/4

1/4   1/4   1/4

1/4 + 1/4 + 1/4 = 3/4

Take one more muffin for a friend. The fraction is 3/4.

That leaves 1/4 of the
muffins on the plate.

Or does it?

Words You Know

1/2   1/2

fraction

muffins

part

Index

About the Author

Dr. Townsend is a teacher, a writer, and an editor. She likes apples and apple muffins. Her recipe for apple muffins uses fractions.

Photo Credits